MW00960612

ALPACAS

The Ultimate Guide To Alpacas Care, Feeding, Housing, Training (Complete Alpacas Information)

Amani Barton

Table of Contents

CHAPTER ONE

Alpaca

They are not related to sheep or any of the other more familiar "Old World" domestic animals, despite their cute appearance (which includes a gangly neck and legs, sharp ears, cleft toes, and a super-soft coat). They are, in fact, South American and hail from the "New World" (although such designations seem a little redundant at this point). They are the domesticated form of the wild vicua, a species closely related to the llama.

Llamas and guanacos are bigger and have rougher coats than their smaller, more refined relatives, the alpacas and vicuas. They're all related since they share the Camelid family name with camels and dromedaries, two additional relatives.

There are striking parallels between South American camelids and their African and Asian relatives, despite the absence of humps in the former. When you examine their face, you will see this to be particularly true. They all have the same long neck, two-toed feet, and large, sad eyes.

There is a lot of overlap in our relationships with them. Historically, Camelids have served a variety of functions, including as pack animals, sources of meat, and fibre producers; those native to South America, in particular, are prized for the exceptional quality of the coat fibers they produce. In particular, alpacas and vicuas generate an extremely fine and delicate fiber that is constructed significantly differently from sheep's wool. Hypoallergenic, very insulating, and incredibly kitty-soft, it is used alone or in combination with other fibers to create yarn and textiles. Baby alpacas (known as crias) have the softest fur you'll ever feel on their first downy hair on their snout.

Domesticated from the wild South American camel, the vicua (Vicugna vicugna), the alpaca (Vicugna pacos) is a member of the family Camelidae (order Artiodactyla) and a near relative of the llama (Lama glama) and the guanaco (Lama guanicoe). The alpaca's range extends from the southern regions of Colombia and Ecuador to the northern regions of Chile and Argentina, where they are found in the wetter, mountainous regions of those countries. They have a long neck and legs, a short tail, a tiny head, and huge, pointy ears, yet their bodies are quite lean.

Of the four species of lamoids, alpacas are the most specialized and have the narrowest range requirements, since they can only survive in wet environments between 4,000 and 4,800 meters in elevation (13,000 to 15,700 feet). Unlike llamas, which may grow to be over two meters tall, alpacas typically top out at 90 centimeters (35 inches) at the shoulder and weigh between 55 and 65 kilograms (121 to 143 pounds). The alpaca's body is rounder than that of the llama's, and the alpaca, unlike the llama, tends to keep its tail pressed against its body rather than maintaining it upright. Aside from the more common black and brown, the alpaca's shaggy coat may be found in a wide range of other colors, including gray, tan, pale yellow, and even white.

habitats inhabited by camels

The alpaca's background has been hotly contested for decades. The fact that alpacas and llamas may mate and have productive offspring together muddied the waters of this discussion by suggesting that both species likely descended from guanacos. Llamas descended from guanacos. Genetic research undertaken in the early 21st century, however, established that alpacas are the domesticated offspring of vicuas and that this domestication happened in the Andes Mountains around 6,000 to 7,000 years ago.

When it comes to the production of wool, alpacas are far and by the most significant lamo species. Only the nobles and monarchy of the Incan Empire were permitted to wear robes woven from precious alpaca and vicua fleeces. The huacaya and the suri are two of the alpaca breeds that originated in the Americas before the arrival of the Spanish. When left unshorn, a suri's silky, delicate fleece may reach the floor. The huacaya's fleece is rougher and much shorter. (For details, see premium hair fiber.) The fleece of an alpaca is renowned for its exceptional qualities: it is not only very lightweight, but also incredibly durable, glossy, highly insulating, and resistant to wet and snowy conditions. It's a common material for linings of parkas, sleeping bags, and high-end outerwear. Dress and lightweight suit fabrics, as well as pile textiles used for coating and lining, may be crafted from alpaca fiber. The city of Arequipa serves as a major hub for the marketing of Peru's famous fleece. The government of Peru has launched a breeding program to boost the quantity and quality of alpaca fleece.

Suris alpacas produce fine fleeces weighing around 3 kg (6.5 pounds) per animal during shearing, whereas huacaya alpacas produce coarser fleeces weighing about 2.5 kg (5.5 pounds) at shearing (5.5 pounds). In two years, a huacaya's hair will have grown around 30 centimeters (12 inches), while a suri's will have grown about 60 centimeters (23.6 inches). At the time of shearing, the length of individual fibers in the fleece varies between around 20 and 40 cm (7.9 and 15.7 inches). The average lifespan of an alpaca is between 15 and 20 years.

Domesticating alpacas, which are related to camels, began 6,000 years ago in the Peruvian Andes, where they were used for food, fuel, and fiber. They are members of the order of giant hoofed mammals known as ungulates, which also includes sheep and giraffes. These animals have enormous bodies and legs, long necks, tiny heads, and rather long fluffy tails. Alpacas are related to llamas but may easily be distinguished from them because to their shorter ears and blunter, although nonetheless endearing, features.

The fleecy coats of alpacas are highly sought after because they can be sheared to create warm, soft, lightweight fabrics. They have a wide array of coat colors, with 22 different possibilities. While they are cultivated in many countries throughout the world, including Australia, the United States, and the United Kingdom, their natural habitat is the Andes Mountains, which stretch from Bolivia and Colombia all the way down to Peru, Ecuador, and Argentina.

Both the Huacaya and the Suri alpaca are popular as household pets. Ninety percent of the world's alpacas are huacaya, which are known for their crimped, compact, and velvety fleece. The remainder of the alpaca population are Suris, whose coats have a corkscrew look due to their longer fibers and silkier texture. Once a year, before the weather gets too hot, they receive a good shearing.

Alpaca sexes seem quite identical to one another. The males are bulkier and have bigger, more pronounced fangs (canine and incisor teeth).

These teeth, which may measure more than an inch in length, are unusual in herbivores but not unheard of.

CHAPTER TWO

Habits and eating habits

While alpacas' claws are sharp, their feet are cushioned and soft enough that they don't damage the grass. They only consume grass, which they find in the Andes Mountains and Valleys. Alpacas are sociable creatures who need the company of at least one other alpaca to flourish; as a result, they are often maintained in herds but also sometimes as companion animals or pets.

They communicate via a wide range of calls, some of which

might indicate more than one thing. A query is indicated by an alpaca's high-pitched hum, whereas a deeper hum, known as a "status hum," may be an indication of satisfaction, stress, or discomfort. Mild hostility may be conveyed by noises like a snort, cluck, or click. The warning cry of alpacas is unmistakable due to its high-pitched, piercing whistle.

Male alpacas reach sexual maturity at the 2.5-year mark, which is also when they begin reproducing. Females are sexually mature around 10–12 months of age, but are often not bred until they are 2 years old and weigh about half as much as they would at full adult size. That's because delivery complications are more common in females with smaller frames.

The Andes are their natural habitat, where mating occurs at certain times of the year. Outside of that zone, people can have babies whenever they choose. When a female indicates she is receptive, the male will follow her until she assumes the cush or kush posture, where her legs are tucked beneath her.

Female alpacas don't ovulate at regular intervals throughout their reproductive cycles, and after they've mated, they may aggressively refuse male approaches, which might be a sign that she's pregnant.

On average, a pregnancy lasts 342 days, although it may last up to a year. However, alpaca pregnancies aren't usually noticeable, even in the latter stages. Females only have one offspring, a cria, and it is able to take its first steps soon after birth. About 90% of crias are born during the day, and they average between 12 and 15 pounds at birth. By the time they turn one, they've put on around a hundred pounds since being weaned at six months.

Conservation

All alpacas are domesticated and have been for the last 6,000 years, however they have not been assessed by the International Union for the Conservation of Nature. In the 16th century, when the Spanish invaded South America, they killed out 90% of the animal population. One of its closest surviving wild relatives is the vicua, the smallest of the camel family and a native of western and central South America. While llamas originated from another camel relative—the guanaco—alpacas were domesticated from vicunas.

Climate change is a major danger to the world's alpaca population since it is altering the Andean region's traditional weather patterns, where these animals traditionally graze. Drying out and weather fluctuations have left the previously lush pastures at their 13,000 foot heights susceptible to disease.

One other danger to the alpaca population is hybridization with llamas and vicua. According to research published in the Journal of Arid Environments in 2020, the ancestral DNA of alpacas are becoming diluted as a result of crossbreeding among species of the camel families of South America.

But it seems to have flourished in areas where it has been cultivated. The first Andean alpacas arrived in the United States in 1984, and now there are more than 250,000 of them here. Almost all of the four million alpacas in the world are located in Peru and Bolivia.

CHAPTER THREE

Is there a particular reason you want an alpaca as a house pet?

As they can adapt to a wide variety of climates, alpacas are very versatile and need little in the way of maintenance or attention from their owners. Because alpacas are so docile and friendly with kids, they make great picnic companions when leashed up and brought along. Some people may find it convenient because alpacas consistently eliminate and urinate in the same locations. similar to how we think of cats with their litter boxes. When compared to other common pets like dogs, rabbits, and guinea pigs, an alpaca's lifetime of 15 to 20 years gives you a little more time to bond with your new best friend. As an added bonus, you can get them in many different hues. The Australian Alpaca Association has recognized 12 color families, giving you a wide range of options.

Before we get started

Even though alpacas are tamed, they are still livestock and not like your regular dogs and cats.

You may be looking at the incorrect pet if you anticipate plenty of cozy encounters. Rarely will an alpaca come up and cuddle with you. All alpacas are kind, although some won't stay still long enough to be handled. To bond with this creature, you must be patient. Let them come to you at their own speed and don't interrupt them if they're in the middle of something important.

That's right; they're known to spit and kick. These aren't planned attacks, however. They're only reacting defensively, and they only do so when they feel threatened. They spit at each other more often than people do, especially when they are scared, trying to establish dominance, or if a female alpaca is pregnant and trying to avoid sexual attention from a male alpaca.

It's crucial that you, as the owner, remember the standard maintenance they need. To provide just one example, much like domesticated canines and felines, alpacas need regular checkups and preventative care for parasites. Vaccinating alpacas is similar to how sheep are vaccinated twice yearly with a "5-in-1" vaccine, but there are several differences. In addition to basic care, such as nail clipping and shearing, they also need regular foot care. If you want to make sure your pet is always safe and healthy, it's best to talk to your vet about what steps you need to take and when.

It has been said that alpacas get along nicely with cats and other livestock. While dogs are often employed as guard animals to protect sheep and goats from predators, the presence of dogs may cause anxiety and fear in alpacas. Frequently, they will stomp, which might hurt your dog. The converse is also possible, with cases of alpacas being injured by dogs. Putting up a fence or leashing up your dog to take things gently is recommended if you have a pet dog. Keep an eye out for any pets that could belong to your neighbors.

Let's say a friend of yours is willing to give you a male cria alpaca since his mother didn't want him. Your internal monologue may have included the thought, "Score! This cria I received is really adorable! ". You've been spending so much time with him that he's become more harsh and aggressive as he's grown bigger while you've been spending so much time with him in bed, playing, and bottle feeding him.

The "berserk male syndrome" occurs when a cria is coddled and handled too much, leading the cria to believe that you, too, are an alpaca. Innocent and cute while the cria is young, but these behaviors might become harmful to you and your alpaca if you're not careful. This means you shouldn't pet a male cria like you would a dog. Any inappropriate behavior in crias must be dealt with quickly.

Increase it by 100%

Being social creatures by design, alpacas can't handle being alone for long periods of time and even end up dying as a result. It's real, although it seems a little fantastic and fanciful at first. As a result, a minimum of two is suggested so that people may have company.

CHAPTER FOUR

Is that still a viable option?

The correct response is "Yes, it can," but there is a catch. The most important thing is preparation. Make sure you have all the essentials, such as what they need in terms of living quarters, companionship, diet, and safety precautions. It is helpful to have a camelid vet in the region when getting your first alpaca. Also, to help out in case any problems come up. Taking care of an alpaca as a pet is a huge commitment. Consequently, you should determine whether an alpaca is the right pet for you and maintain reasonable expectations.

In general, llamas and alpacas are docile creatures.

They are social creatures that do best in groups; their prey animal instincts make them vigilant, yet easily startled. Their attitude is often shown by spitting at the danger, which may be quite off-putting. But if you treat them well and interact with them often, they will grow sociable and less likely to spit at the first sign of a stranger or an unfamiliar sound in their paddocks. A halter should be trained on them, and they should be handled often to maintain the habit. This improves the quality of care provided in the event of an emergency or during normal checkups by making encounters less stressful and more secure.

Alpacas, like other camelids, are well-known for their vigilant herd protection, and they are frequently content to watch after flocks of sheep or other small domestic animals. They will follow the prey, hiss and spit at them, kick them, and create such a ruckus that the predator will likely abandon the area in search of easier prey. Mixing 3–4 alpacas in the lambing field and allowing them keep a watch on comings and goings has been shown to effectively protect lambs from foxes, crows, and even badgers.

Or should we call them pests?

Because of their size and aggressive nature, alpacas and other Camelids may be hazardous animals for anyone who aren't familiar with them. As a result, only mature, knowledgeable individuals should handle them, and kids should never be left alone with any animal.

Although cattle typically do not spread many zoonotic illnesses (zoonotic = contagious to humans), bovine tuberculosis stands out as the most prominent and potentially deadly in the UK (bTB). The susceptibility of camelids to this illness is quite high. Sadly, there have been reports of their spreading the disease to other cattle and even humans.

Those who own alpacas should be familiar with the Animal and Plant Health Agency's (APHA) current requirements for bTB management in camelids. Always consult your local veterinarian and the APHA for the most recent information.

Alpacas don't fit the typical profile of a nuisance. They aren't a nuisance since they don't destroy crops or enter barns. They're more easily kept in their pastures than many kinds of sheep or goats.

Even though intact males during the time of breeding may become sexual pests to all of the females in their herd, a responsible owner who has no interest in reproducing would have them castrated. All animals, no matter how big or little, need careful, attentive, and knowledgeable caretakers, therefore it's always best to arm yourself with this information before bringing any new creatures into your farm.

Informatives about alpacas

- They are classified as a functional ruminant due to their habit of chewing the cud, but they are not ruminants on the basis of anatomy since they lack a rumen.

- The term "kush" is used to describe the posture in which they lay on their bellies while chewing the cud, with their legs tucked neatly beneath them.

- A cria is the name for a newborn llama or alpaca (crias in plural).

- Giving birth is a kind of "unpacking" (as opposed to lambing or calving in sheep and cattle).

- The gender-specific terms for females, "hembra," and males, "macho," are used. One definition of a maiden is an unbred woman.

- A cria's mother carries her young for roughly 11 months (give or take a few weeks). Since the cria can only nurse for the first time after they are up and walking, the mother emits mild sounds (a form of humming) to encourage them to get up and move about soon after birth. Unlike cows, who lick and push their calves in all directions to get them going, alpaca moms typically just hang about and keep an eye out for danger, softly nudging the cria with their nose and humming to encourage bonding.

They are known for their loud voices and friendly nature. Hear some real-life recordings of llama and alpaca bleating and nickering

Conclusions Regarding the Acquisition of a Llama or an Alpaca

Keeping a llama or alpaca as a pet isn't everyone's idea of a good time, but it may be worthwhile if you have the room and time for it. Shearing him once a year may also provide enough profit to cover the cost of owning one. Either animal is essential to have if you have sheep since they both help to keep the flock secure. The affection you feel for them will be reciprocated in spades. Llamapaedia is also an excellent resource for learning how to take care of a llama or alpaca as a pet.

THE END

Made in the USA
Las Vegas, NV
09 March 2024

86960470R00026